Understanding Boat Refrigeration and Air Conditioning Systems

OTHER BOOKS BY JOHN C. PAYNE

The Fisherman's Electrical Manual

The Great Cruising Cookbook: an International Galley Guide

Marine Electrical and Electronics Bible, Third Edition

Motorboat Electrical and Electronics Manual

Piracy Today: Fighting Villainy on the High Seas

Understanding Boat AC Power Systems

Understanding Boat Batteries and Battery Charging

Understanding Boat Communications

Understanding Boat Corrosion, Lightning Protection and Interference

Understanding Boat DC Electrical Equipment

Understanding Boat Diesel Engines

Understanding Boat Electronics

Understanding Boat Plumbing and Water Systems

Understanding Boat Wiring

Understanding Boat Refrigeration and Air Conditioning Systems

John C. Payne

SHERIDAN HOUSE

This edition first published 2010 by
Sheridan House Inc.
145 Palisade Street,
Dobbs Ferry, NY 10522

Library of Congress Cataloging-in-Publication Data

Payne, John C.
    Understanding boat refrigeration and air conditioning systems /
John C. Payne.
        p. cm.
    ISBN 978-1-57409-300-1
        1. Marine refrigeration—Handbooks, manuals, etc. 2. Boats and
boating—Air conditioning—Handbooks, manuals, etc. 3. Ships—
Air conditioning—Handbooks, manuals, etc. I. Title.
    VM485.P39 2010
    623.8'53—dc22   2010038850

Printed in the United States of America

ISBN 978-1-57409-300-1

CONTENTS

1. Refrigeration
1

a. System Selection

b. Refrigeration Principles

c. Eutectic Refrigeration Systems

d. Electric Refrigeration Systems

e. Refrigeration Troubleshooting

2. Ice Makers
51

3. Air Conditioning
55

4. Heating Systems
67

5. Ventilation Systems
75

1. REFRIGERATION

They say a boat runs on its stomach and so that includes a well-found galley to keep the crew happy. And of course that means efficient refrigeration is central to providing good quality meals. Properly functioning refrigeration systems also include ice making systems. The refrigeration system must be properly selected, installed and maintained. This book illustrates the basic principles of refrigeration and the most common systems found on both sailing and motor boats.

I once served as Electrical Officer/Engineer on some of the most automated and advanced refrigerated cargo ships afloat. We were carrying beef, lamb, chicken, bananas, apples and grapes. The multi-compressor refrigeration and computerized control systems required a great deal of maintenance.

For those who need to know: On the Fahrenheit scale, the freezing point is 32°F, and the boiling point is 212°F. On the Celsius scale the freezing point is zero 0°C and boiling point 100°C. Conversion is °C = ⅝ x °F, or °F = ⅝ x °C.

A. SYSTEM SELECTION

The two main choices are a mechanical driven or an electrical powered system. Several factors must be considered when choosing a system.

Battery demand

Electric refrigeration systems are relatively power hungry. No matter how many systems put forward attractive consumption figures (and most are quoted in ideal conditions), the average usage is around 50 amp-hours for a refrigerator, and around 100 amp-hours for freezers on a 50% duty cycle. The demand varies with a number of factors that include the climate you are sailing in, the insulation quality and more.

Battery charging

A far greater run time is required to restore battery capacity than for an equivalent engine driven system. You will definitely require a higher output alternator, and an alternator fast-charging regulator is essential. The average vessel recharging time with electric systems is typically around one hour, morning and night. Remember that you have to replace 120% of the power used from the battery.

Power efficiency

The majority of electric systems now use hermetically sealed, Danfoss-type compressors. The reciprocating compressor system is far more efficient, more reliable and robust. It is almost universally found on engine driven and DC motor powered systems. An engine driven compressor applies a greater load to the engine, which along with an alternator and a fast-charge device, allows reasonably economical engine use. One advantage of an electric system is that it keeps temperatures stable over a long period, so the actual run times to pull down temperatures are relatively small.

Mechanical system costs

The mechanical engine driven system is generally more expensive to install, requires more engineering, pipework, etc. Engine maintenance is lower than simple battery charging duties because the run times have greater loads and are for considerably shorter periods. Engine driven compressors make more economical use of the engine by imposing a substantial load, which reduces engine maintenance costs. If you have to run the engine for battery charging, it makes good sense to fully utilize the energy source. The extra load also gets the water hot if you have a calorifier.

Electrical system costs

Electric systems are initially cheaper to buy and install. They often just need to be plugged in but they do require much greater battery capacity, and much money can be spent on solar and wind systems, high output alternators, etc. Also, longer engine run times are often required when wind and sun do not deliver, generally costing more in maintenance and fuel. Where there is sufficient charging capabilities or AC power, or long marina dockside time it is quite easy to install AC electrically powered systems. They suit the weekend and day sailor.

Dual engine and electric systems

An engine driven system enables both refrigerator and freezer to run off the same refrigeration plant. There is a growing trend to incorporate engine driven compressors with small electric systems. That means two different system holding plates. The main refrigerator space can be pulled down initially and every second day using the engine compressor. The electric unit, sustained by alternative energy sources, can then maintain the temperature for a significantly increased period.

Choosing a system

If you are doing an ice chest conversion or are about to choose a new refrigeration system there are many factors that you need to consider.

The first big question on which everything else is based is how big an ice chest you are installing. This also entails considering whether it's just for standard refrigeration or as a freezer box.

Are you planning offshore cruising or local weekend sailing? The answer will have big implications for the system you install and will also impact the budget you allocate for the project. If you are sailing to sunnier and warmer tropical places, insulation values also become a factor.

How to power the system? Bigger boats have AC generators and this allows the use of AC systems. If you want high powered systems you might choose a compressor driven off your propulsion engine. You might also want to look at a 12 volt DC powered system. This impacts the battery capacity installed and related charging system.

If you choose an electrical system over a mechanical one, it can be 110 VAC, 220 VAC or a 12 VDC hermetic type. Also the question of air cooled or water cooled then comes into the equation.

B. REFRIGERATION PRINCIPLES

The fundamental principle is that when a high-pressure liquid or gas expands, the temperature reduces. In a refrigeration system, a compressor pumps the refrigerant fluid around the system. The typical cycle of a system is as follows:

Compression phase

The compressor pumps the refrigerant vapor. This increases the refrigerant gas pressure, which becomes very hot. The high-pressure superheated gas then passes through to the condenser.

Condensation phase

The hot gas passes through a condenser, which acts as a heat exchanger and releases or rejects the heat. The condenser is either air cooled by natural convection, or by a fan, or by water passing through the coils. The gas condenses back into a hot liquid and travels to the thermal expansion valve. The liquid may then go to a receiver. The receiver is essentially a pressure vessel that maintains the refrigerant in a liquid state before passing it through an expansion valve.

Refrigerant control

The thermostatic expansion valve (TX valve) regulates the rate of refrigerant liquid flow from the liquid receiver high side into the evaporator low side. It also maintains the pressure difference and therefore expansion into the evaporator is in exact proportion to the rate of liquid leaving the evaporator.

The flow is regulated in response to both pressure and temperature within the evaporator. The thermal sensing element is placed on the outlet end of the evaporator and where installed also a motor thermal sensing element, which consists of a bulb and capillary. Valves can normally be adjusted for optimum temperature.

This pressure reduction causes a fall in temperature of the liquid. The cold liquid changes to a low pressure saturated gas which then passes to the evaporator. The thermostatic expansion valve is controlled by two factors, the temperature of the control element and the evaporator pressure. Automatic TX valves allow refrigerant flow only if the evaporator pressure falls when the compressor operates. The single greatest cause of TX valve failure is dirt, acids, moisture and sludge in the system. All of these will freeze up or jam the valve.

Evaporation phase

The low pressure saturated gas changes to a cool dry gas that passes through to the evaporator cooling surfaces (or on some boats the eutectic tanks). Heat within the refrigerator space is absorbed by the cold refrigerant causing the air to cool and chilling the food or beverages. The warm air evaporates the liquid part of the refrigerant mixture. The refrigerant then is suctioned back into the compressor to repeat the cycle and the heat is later rejected in the condenser.

Figure 1-1 Basic Refrigeration Cycle

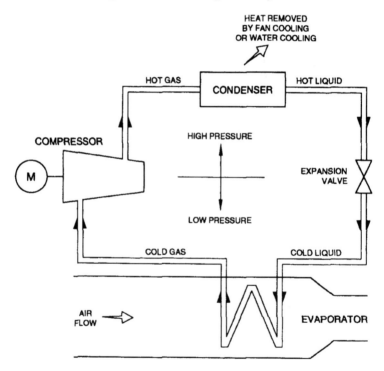

Figure 1-2 Electric Refrigeration System

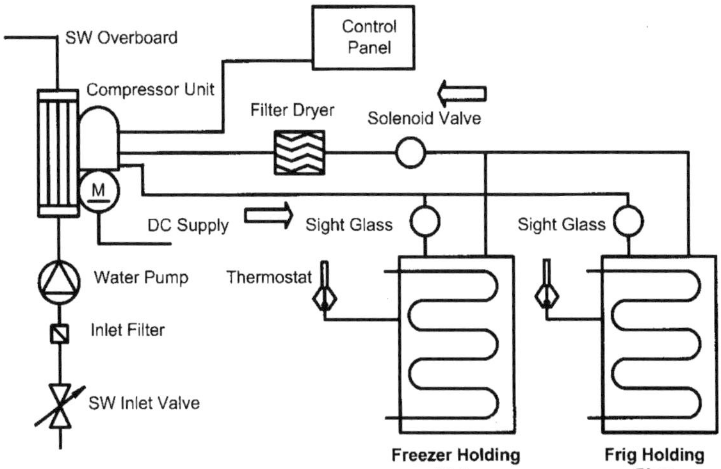

SW Overboard

Control Panel

Compressor Unit

Filter Dryer

Solenoid Valve

M

DC Supply

Sight Glass

Sight Glass

Water Pump

Thermostat

Inlet Filter

SW Inlet Valve

Freezer Holding Plate

Frig Holding Plate

The dryer

There will always be a small amount of water vapor remaining in a system regardless of purging and evacuation. Water causes ice formation at the expansion valve creating either total blockage or bad operation. The dryer is installed in the liquid line between the receiver and expansion valve serving as both a filter and removing water.

The dryer desiccant materials are made of silica gel or activated alumina. Flared units enable easy change-out when saturated, rather than soldered units and the removable cartridge types are even better. Internal corrosion begins at above 15ppm of water, which also causes oil breakdown making it acidic, and contributing to premature motor burnouts in hermetic systems. A suction accumulator is used to prevent liquid slugging to the compressor.

The sight glass

The sight glass allows visual inspection of the refrigerant liquid. It is installed between the dryer/filter and the expansion valve. A sight glass also usually incorporates a moisture indicator.

Bubbles within the sight glass indicate low refrigerant levels. There is a moisture indicator that changes color. Green indicates the system is dry, yellow/green is used to indicate caution and yellow indicates it is wet. Some indicators also go from blue for dry to pink when wet.

The site glass will sometimes show bubbles if refrigerant is low. Often this is seen at start-up and stop of the system. Bubbles also may mean the refrigerant is partially evaporating within the liquid line. It will also show restrictions or blocked filter dryers ahead of the sight glass. Water in the system can cause corrosion, chemical damage, and damage to the compressors. Be aware that at start up the indicator may show wet. It may take 12 hours of running to stabilize and show dry. If it doesn't you need to act and get the system repaired. Usually the dryer will need changing.

Refrigerants

The most common refrigerant used to be Freon 12 (R12), but as it is harmful to the ozone layer, like all CFC gases it has been replaced. HFC-134a has become the new standard refrigeration system gas. This gas type was an obvious choice since auto air conditioning systems use the same gas, having already made the conversion. Virtually all manufacturers now have efficient HFC-134a systems on the market.

There are many refrigerants in use that include R12, R22, R134a, R 502, R113, R407c, R401a, R507, R410a, etc. The earlier and common CFC gases such as R12, R22 or HCFC22 are now almost phased out. R410a has replaced R22.

As of July 1, 1992 it is illegal to release refrigerants into the atmosphere, either intentionally or accidentally. These gases can cause severe damage to the ozone layer. The EPA and the CAA (Clean Air Act) have strict rules and regulations. The rules cover recycling, recovery, reclaiming, etc. Sales of refrigerant are restricted to certified technicians. People servicing or disposing of refrigerants are required to certify to the EPA that they have acquired refrigerant recovery. There are many rules to comply with now. Do-it-yourself is no longer allowed.

C. EUTECTIC REFRIGERATION SYSTEMS

This is the most common and efficient method of vessel refrigeration, especially on cruising yachts. The evaporator is replaced by a eutectic plate or tank.

Eutectic holding plates have often been associated with mechanical engine driven compressors. The major attraction of eutectic holding plates is that they store thermal energy and hold over the ice chest space until the next scheduled refrigeration cycle. This is very energy efficient for battery or engine powered systems. The aluminium evaporator will have to run constantly to maintain ice chest temperatures so it is not efficient. This is only viable in large boats with constant generator power supplies.

Basic eutectic principles

A eutectic system uses brine or a fluid that freezes at what is called eutectic temperature. Originally brine solutions were used but systems now have an ethylene glycol/water mixture or similar. The mixture has a much lower freezing point than water which is 0°C. Once the mixture is frozen completely (at the eutectic point) and refrigeration is removed, the tank will cool the refrigeration space, gradually thawing out as it absorbs heat.

Holdover period

The period of time that the ice chest space will remain within the required temperature ranges before refrigeration is required is called the holdover period. When specifying a system, the holdover time and the temperature required are critical to the size of the plates or tanks and of the type of eutectic solution required.

Air or water cooling?

Which works best, water or air cooling, is often debated. The key to efficient air cooling is good ventilation to carry the heat away. Water cooling is equally effective but it has its challenges. In many cases the air cooled unit is boxed into a small space with inadequate ventilation and system performance is reduced making water cooling a viable option.

If water cooling is considered, there are two alternatives, pump or keel cooling. The keel cooler seen on systems is typically a 3 inch x 7 inch bronze plate that is located on the hull exterior. This type of heat exchanger is ideal for larger refrigerator spaces and freezers. This type of cooler does not require a pump and is virtually silent. The conventional condenser cooler uses an electric water pump, some use seawater to cool a close loop fresh water system. This type of system requires more plumbing, higher maintenance with strainers and also pumps.

Isotherm has developed an innovative new system, called the self-pumping (SP) cooling system. A special integrated condenser and through-hull fitting have been developed that replace the galley sink fitting. The movement of the vessel causes the water to pump in and out and remove waste heat. This is a great idea because pumps and fans are eliminated with far greater efficiency in heat transfer.

Compressors and motors

There are five compressor types in common use on eutectic systems, the reciprocating, rotary, scroll, screw and centrifugal. Many systems use an engine driven reciprocating compressor, or either DC or AC motor powered compressors with a belt drive. Engine powered units have a belt drive off the engine and the drive pulley has an electromagnetic clutch for operation of the compressor. The most common compressors in use are the reciprocating and swash plate types.

Compressor DC drive motors

Glacier Bay DC motor systems have quoted figures for power consumption over 24 hours at 20.5 amp-hours and 39.5 amp-hours for refrigerator and freezer respectively. DC drive motors are typically rated at ½ horsepower, and Leeson is the most common. Glacier Bay developed a new LS (Low Speed) motor which operates at lower speed 675 rpm rather than the 1800 rpm Leeson. With 300% greater torque it is nearly 80% heavier. Unlike the Leeson unit with 2 pole magnets and 2 brushes it has 6 poles and 4 brushes and is designed to have an increased service life of 500%. Other features are the ventilated commutator and significantly reduced running temperatures.

D. ELECTRIC REFRIGERATION SYSTEMS

DC motor direct-driven electric systems

Some refrigeration units use a heavy-duty DC motor and compressor. Like all systems, they use 134a gas and are very compact. Cooling is accomplished by using a water jacket to remove condenser, compressor, and motor heat.

DC motor belt-driven electric systems

Belt tension must be regularly checked. These systems often have a thermostat bypass switch so that during engine runs, maximum pull-down is achieved.

DC motor driven system maintenance

If you have a brush type motor and not one of the newer permanent magnet type DC motors, you need to perform maintenance.

Every 3 months, check and clean the DC motor commutator, use a vacuum cleaner to remove dust, and then if very dirty wash down the brush-gear with an electrical cleaner. Ensure that brushes move freely within brush holders. Tighten all electrical connections.

Compressor brackets

The engine compressor mountings and brackets must be extremely robust to prevent vibration. You must make sure that vibration will not fracture any part of it.

Compressor drive belts

Alignment of the compressor and engine drive pulleys is essential to ensure proper transfer of mechanical loads. Belts are usually dual pulley arrangements. Ensure that both belts are tensioned correctly.

Swash plate compressors

These are typified by automotive air conditioning compressors and are satisfactory where temperatures down to approximately minus 15°C are required. They are suitable for most average applications. These compressors are not really designed for eutectic refrigeration systems and although they work well, failure rates are higher than reciprocating units. They are ideal in air conditioning applications.

Reciprocating compressors

The reciprocating compressor consists of cylinders, piston intake and exhaust valves, and connecting rods to the crankshaft similar to an engine. The compressors are driven by belts from the drive motors.

Daily Checks

Check the operating pressure gauges, temperatures, compressor oil levels, and abnormal noise or vibration.

Weekly Checks

Check the evaporator and defrost if necessary. Check that all valve covers are on and tight.

Bi-annual Checks

Check the operation of high and low pressure cut-out switches. Perform an oil sample test (for water). Inspect and clean the condenser. Check the rubber V-belts and adjust.

Lubrication

Lubricants in use within refrigeration systems are called miscible, wax free oils. They do not degrade under low temperatures or high pressures. Lubricating oils are carried around the system with the refrigerant and eventually return back to the compressor sump. It should be noted that only reciprocating compressors have an oil sump, while swash plate units do not.

On reciprocating compressors always check the oil levels. Oil should be shiny and clear, have no visible particles, and feel smooth and greasy when rubbed between the fingers. If in doubt, renew the oil. Sample analysis will help determine internal component condition and wear. Wear particles should not exceed in parts per million (ppm) the following values: Lead (10); Copper (10); Silicon (25); Iron (100); Chrome (5); Nickel (5); Aluminum (10) and Tin (10).

More about lubrication

Having the right refrigeration lubrication oils is essential but there are things to understand.

Alkylbenzene is a synthetic aromatic hydro-carbon lubricant oil. Mineral oil is compatible with this and can be used with the majority of refrigeration gases but this excludes 134a. The vast majority of AC hermetic refrigeration compressors use alkylbenzene.

Polyol Ester oil is required for R134a refrigerant systems. This lubricant is also compatible with R12, R22 and also 502 refrigerant gases.

Mineral oil is a wax-free oil and has been the de-facto standard lubricant within refrigeration systems for many years. When in a Freon 12 mixture it migrates completely through the entire refrigeration system, but it will not mix with R134a refrigerants.

Polyalkylene Glycol (PAG) is often used in automobiles. It should not be considered for refrigeration conversions as it is completely incompatible with all other refrigeration lubrication oils.

Reciprocating compressor servicing

Perform the following maintenance routines:

> **Condenser Pressure and Temperature.** High pressures indicate reduced cooling or air in the condenser. Low pressures indicate that the refrigerant may be restricted to the evaporator.
>
> **Filters.** Liquid line, oil return, suction line and TX valve require cleaning, as clogged filters will cause restrictions in evaporator supply.
>
> **Moisture Indicators.** If these alter from green to yellow moisture is in the system and filter dryer requires replacement.
>
> **Leak Detection.** Regular checks should be made on new installation every month until joints and flanges settle, and are retightened. Refrigerant should be recharged as required.
>
> **Pressure Switches.** These should be checked and adjusted.
>
> **Condensers.** Open and clean the tubes, as it is quite common to have a blocked or fouled tube. Check and replace the anodes where installed.
>
> **Rubber Drive Belts.** Rubber V-belts should be checked and re-tensioned regularly.

E. REFRIGERATION TROUBLESHOOTING

Compressor Abnormal Noises

Low oil pressure—check the oil levels

The oil is foaming

Liquid in the suction line

Coupling misalignment

Oil pump is faulty

Piston ring or cylinder wear within the compressor

Discharge valves are faulty

Solenoid valve on the oil return is faulty

Oil filter is clogged—change the filter

Compressor mounting is loose—tighten the mountings

Low cooling water flow—check the water intakes and pump if used for blockage

High Condenser Pressure

High water temperature

High pressure cut-out is activated

Refrigerant is overcharged

Cooling water loss

High cooling water temperature

Condenser is clogged

Low Condenser Pressure

Inlet water valve is closed

Low refrigerant charge

Excess cooling to condenser

Low Oil Pressure

Piston ring or cylinder wear

Oil pressure switch has activated

Low oil level

Oil pressure is too low at regulator

Oil foaming in crankcase

Liquid in the suction line

Oil pump is defective

Bearings are worn

Oil Level Falling

Oil filter is clogged

Oil is foaming in crankcase

Poor oil return

Liquid in the suction line

Piston rings or cylinders are worn

Solenoid on the oil return is faulty

Reduced or No Cooling

Oil filter is clogged

Leak in the system

Clutch connection is broken

Clutch coil failure

High pressure cut-out has activated

Slow Temperature Pull Down Times

Drive belt is slipping

Low refrigerant level—top up

Compressor fault

High cooling water temperature

Condenser is plugged—open and clean

Low battery voltage—check the charging

Ice chest seals are damaged

High ambient temperature

Ice chest insulation failure

Thermostat is faulty

Clutch Circuit Breaker Tripping

Clutch coil failure

Clutch cable is shorting out—check the wiring at chafe points

Expansion valve is icing up

Compressor bearing failure

Dryer is saturated and requires replacement

Low Oil Temperature

Discharge valves are leaking

Oil level is low—top up the oil

Oil is foaming in crankcase

Oil pump is defective

Bearings are worn

Low Suction Pressure

Oil filter is clogged—change the filter

Oil in the evaporator

Low refrigerant charge—leak test and recharge

TX valve is frozen up

TX valve is not operating

Liquid line filter is clogged

Moisture in System

Liquid line solenoid valve is faulty

Condenser is leaking

Compressor gasket has failed

Refrigerant Gas Leakage

Compressor bearing failure

Pipe compression fitting is loose—a common problem. Check and tighten all of them

Condenser is leaking—may require a pressure test

Isolation valve is leaking

Damaged piping—perform a close visual inspection

Valve caps are off

Hermetic compressors

The majority of electric refrigeration systems use hermetically sealed Danfoss type compressors. The electric motor is sealed within a domed housing along with the compressor. The motor and compressor assembly is supported on a spring suspension system that will absorb vibration. Lubrication and cooling come from oil and refrigerant flowing over the windings. The most common AC motor used in hermetic compressors is the capacitor type. These vary but typically are the capacitor start, induction run type. Condenser and evaporator fans use capacitor and shaded pole type motors.

Hermetic units are mostly twin piston reciprocating compressors with a valve plate assembly. Units with fan driven condenser cooling should be cleaned every 3 months. Tube flare nuts and service valve caps should be tight to prevent leaks. These compressors are rather old in concept. They were initially used by General Electric back in 1926 for household refrigerators and have kept most kitchens running since then. The new Danfoss DC compressors use a brushless motor without all of the maintenance dependent brush and commutator arrangements. They incorporate an electronic control unit and 3-phase winding.

The Isotherm Magnum ASU unit is a hermetically sealed, pre-charged 134a system. Having installed a unit on my last boat I am pleased with the performance. The units are easy to install and have water cooling, although it is only a low 1.5 liters a minute. An important innovation is the automatic compressor motor speed function. Upon detection of a higher voltage on the supply, from alternator or battery charger, the electronics module operates the motor at double speed, ensuring a quick pull-down of the holdover plate while power is available, and then it reverts to economy mode.

With a small refrigerator/freezer compartment, I opted for a freezer model with spill-over plate and stainless butterfly vent to adjust cooling in the refrigerator space. Note that the seawater cooling system anode must be removed every 6 months and cleaned, or it will shed enough material to clog the pump suction lines. My own solution is to install a separate valve in the seawater inlet with a small 2-liter bottle. When shutting down for any period, simply flush the system with fresh water. In cold climates, remember to add antifreeze.

Danfoss compressors

The Danfoss Model BD2, BD2.5 and BD3 compressors types are by far the most common types in use. They are rapidly being displaced by Model BD35 types. These compressors have multispeed and they offer refrigeration designers and manufacturers a range of options. The compressor speed is set to match the absorption rate of the evaporator.

At its highest speed it runs at 35,000 rpm and at the lowest speed at 2,000 rpm. The BD35 compressor is speed variable. This is achieved by the addition of resistance inserted into the thermostat circuit, so at 2,000 rpm there is no resistance and the speed increases as resistance is added.

The Danfoss BD50F compressor is also an option for higher performance warm and tropical climate installations and where larger ice chests are used. These compressors typically get 100,000 hours of service life and better.

Danfoss compressor speed control

Ensuring maximum efficiency when the main engine and DC alternator are on and charging the batteries is very desirable. I elected to install an Isotherm ASU (Automatic Speed Up) unit on one of my boats. The idea was for the automatic controller to detect the higher charge voltage and then increase compressor speed and so utilize the charging source. I found it to be very effective. Frigoboat also have what is called Smart Speed Control (SSC).

Energy utilization

Some manufacturers have introduced circuitry that enables the over-riding of thermostats during engine run periods. If temperatures are down, the alternator can supply loads for an additional pull down period that reduces electrical consumption later. A similar function is used on Isotherm ASU (Automatic Start Up) systems. The controller senses the raised system voltage from the alternator and operates at double the speed to pull down temperatures and maximize the available energy. Another feature of Isotherm systems is the control of the compressor speed depending on the refrigeration requirements. New Danfoss hermetically sealed compressors are being used, with electronic control on the three-phase motor supply. In addition, there are also twin compressor models.

Refrigerant charging

You must do some basic steps when recharging your system refrigerant. If you are swapping from R12 or R22 you need to use caution. Always check the refrigerant label on your compressor. You also need to confirm with the compressor manufacturer exactly what refrigerant and what oil should be used.

You must also be aware of certain factors which could create serious problems. Never add 134a to any other type of refrigerant as the mixture will become both toxic and flammable. That means it is not acceptable for any system using mineral or alkybenzene. If you do this it will result in compressor oil starvation and compressor failure.

You should never change out the oil within a hermetic compressor unless the manufacturer approves the replacement. The simple reason is that hermetic compressor motors and the associated cables are normally submerged in the oil and refrigerant mixture. The use of synthetic oils has the potential for dissolving the wiring insulation and causing compressor damage or failure.

If a system has lost all the refrigerant gas you will also need to change the receiver and dryer unit as the system will be contaminated with moisture and air, and these are unacceptable.

After fixing a leak you can go to Kmart, Wal-Mart or many auto parts stores and purchase a recharging kit. They also sell R12 to 134a conversion kits but do not attempt this. It is legal to recharge a 134a system without a license but not R12. It is illegal to open a port and vent the system to check whether gas is present. Before you start make sure the area is well ventilated as gases displace oxygen. 134a is not flammable at normal ambient temperatures but may be at high pressure

You need to identify the service connection points and then attach your refrigerant charging hose to the port located at the low-pressure side if the compressor. Then open the 134a refrigerant can and finally start the refrigeration compressor. Always charge gas from the low-pressure side, never from the high-pressure side. The high pressure side is sometimes marked with the letter H or a red cap. There is a risk that the can could explode.

If you don't understand this, it is best for you to get a refrigeration mechanic to do the job and stay safe. Discharge about 25% of the can into the system and check the system charge levels. Systems that incorporate a sight glass make this relatively easy. Continue to add in the refrigerant in 25% can increments. The compressor should be operated until bubbles are no longer visible within the sight glass. For systems without the site glass, operate the system until normal frosting is seen on the holding plate. Don't overcharge as a pre-emptive step to allow for leaks.

Correct gas charge level

When a refrigeration system is operating at optimum efficiency a light and even layer of frost will be observed on the holding plate.

If a partial frost line is observed, this indicates the system is undercharged.

If frost is observed down the copper refrigeration tubing the system is probably overcharged. To correct this some refrigerant requires gradual releasing (and this is illegal) although many do this. The refrigerant level is okay when the frost has gone.

If moisture is observed on the compressor housing or there is evidence of corrosion and rust this indicates that the system has been either overcharged or undercharged for a considerable period. Also note that a refrigeration compressor that is warm when you touch it may indicate that the refrigeration system is undercharged.

Troubleshooting hermetic compressors

Motor failures due to internal faults are rare. Failures are usually due to external causes. Continuity and resistance checks will indicate status of windings. Start winding C to S resistance is approximately 5 ohms. Run winding C to R resistance is approximately 2 ohms. Both windings R to S resistance is approximately 7 ohms. Megger R or S to case is at least 1 megOhm. Testing of both open circuit voltage and on-load voltage also will indicate problems. A difference exceeding 10 volts indicates an overload or motor winding fault. Use a clamp ammeter to check operating current. If the compressor current draw exceeds 7 amps it is close to failure.

Check all external control devices first before assuming compressor failure. Discharge the capacitor first, and use an ohmmeter (multimeter set) and test across the capacitor terminals. A short circuited capacitor will indicate zero ohms. A high reading indicates an open circuit. If the capacitor is good the reading will initially go to zero then slowly rise. Regular failures in capacitors is usually caused by slow starts (typical maximum is 3–4 seconds), too many starts, (typical rate is 3–4 starts per hours), low supply voltages or starting switches are faulty.

Hermetic compressor system troubleshooting

Compressor Fails to Start (No hum sound)

Power supply has failed or the circuit breaker has tripped

Motor overload device has opened (bridge this out to check)

Relay is defective

Compressor is faulty

Thermostat fault (bridge this out to check)

Wiring connection fault, check and tighten

Capacitor failure

Compressor Fails to Start (humming sound)

Low voltage to the compressor motor

Start relay is faulty

Compressor has an internal fault

Defective start capacitor

Motor winding fault

Compressor Trips Overload

Low voltage to the compressor motor

Motor winding fault

Compressor is seizing

Start relay is not opening

Capacitor Failure

Start relay is faulty

Excessive start period, due to relay fault

Excessive start load current

Excessive short cycling on overload

Compressor Cycle On and Off

Low refrigerant charge

Refrigerant leak

Compressor Runs Continuously

Low refrigerant charge

Refrigerant leak

Thermostat fault

Compressor Stuck

Condenser is dirty

Valve is broken or defective

Compressor overheated

Compressor Short Cycles

Low oil levels

Overload protector is faulty

Thermostat is faulty

Low refrigerant charge

Excess Noise Levels

Air in system

Loose parts, fan or motor vibration

Copper tubing is touching the casing

Compressor or valves have failed

Auxiliary refrigeration controls

A few different control devices are essential for safe and efficient operation.

High Pressure Cut-out Switch

The purpose of the high pressure cut-out is to protect the system against high pressures caused by loss of cooling water, plugged condenser, or in the worst case serious contamination of the refrigerator system with water and air. The cut-out is usually wired in series with the compressor contactor or clutch. Typically this is above 75psi in the condenser. To test operation, close the cooling water off and wait until head pressure builds up and activates it. High pressures can seriously damage refrigeration compressors.

Low Pressure Cut-out Switch

The low-pressure switch monitors suction line pressure. The cut-out operates when gas discharge from the evaporator is too low. Operation of the cut-out is indicative of a low refrigerant charge, typically below 30psi. To test the switch, slowly close in the suction valve to activate the switch. Low suction pressures increase compression ratios and can cause compressor damage.

Thermostats

This is used to sense, set and maintain the required temperatures. To test, vary the settings and observe cut-in and out. Many are now microprocessor controlled and the temperature sensor is located at the holding plate, although some use the general box cooling space. The thermostat controls when the compressor switches on and when it switches off.

The principle of a mechanical thermostat is that sealed capillary tube expands and contracts with temperature. The end is attached to the evaporator and the expansion capillary activates bellows within the thermostat that activates electrical contacts.

Electronic thermostats sense the general ice chest air temperatures. A thermocouple is used to generate a voltage that is processed by the thermostat control circuit. This may be displayed and also a set of contacts activated depending on the set point selection.

Defrost Timers

This is used only on larger vessels where the evaporator has heating elements, and is activated for 1 hour or more every 24 hours. They can malfunction and remain on so regular monitoring is recommended.

Clutch Engine Interlocks

Many electromagnetic clutches are operated from a dedicated circuit breaker on the main switch panel, giving protection on the clutch coil and cabling. It is common for the switch to be inadvertently left on and subsequently flattening the batteries, as typical current draw is around 3–4 amps. On some occasions the operating coil can burn out. To prevent this, an interlock should be installed into the ignition system so that the clutch is de-energized when the engine is shutdown.

Figure 1.3 Refrigeration Clutch Interlock

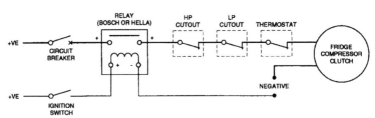

How to save energy

There are a few energy saving, efficiency increasing measures that can be implemented.

> **Void Spaces.** Fill any empty spaces in the refrigerator compartment with blocks of foam or inflated empty wine-cask bladders. This will decrease the refrigerator space and reduce energy requirements.

> **Chest Cooling.** Another useful idea is to install a small fan unit in the chest (Frig-Mate). This should be connected into either the DC compressor circuit or a separate switch. It will enable more rapid displacement of warm air within foodstuffs, and more rapid cooling.

> **Food Covers or Mats.** If all frozen goods are placed at the bottom of the compartment, place a mat over the food so that cold air is retained within the food below the mat.

> **Battery Voltages.** Ensure that battery voltage levels are maintained. Low battery levels will cause inefficient compressor operation. Do not let the battery level sink to the normal minimum level of 10.5 volts. It takes far more energy and engine running time to charge a nearly flat battery than one that is half charged.

> **Ventilation.** See that the compressor unit is well ventilated. Installing a small solar or electric fan will ensure positive ventilation.

Reduced holdover times

A common complaint is that holdover times have reduced for the following reasons:

> **Warm Foodstuffs.** A refrigerator or freezer system is often pulled down to the required temperature and then gets a full load of unfrozen food or warm drinks such as a case of beer dumped in it with the expectation that it will rapidly cool them.

> **Climate Change.** More often than not the system worked well in a temperate climate, but the first extended cruise in tropical waters results in a dramatic reduction in apparent efficiency. A normal boater opens the refrigerator sparingly, but people new to the lifestyle are probably opening it far more than is necessary and far more than they did on a normal weekend cruise. Keep access down to the minimum.

> **Mechanical Causes.** Engine drive belts are not re-tensioned and as such belt slip under load causes decreased refrigeration.

> **Seawater Temperatures.** In many cases where seawater is used for condenser cooling, a voyage to warmer waters also causes changes in condenser cooling efficiency. In many cases the eutectic plate takes longer to pull down, and refrigeration operation times need to be extended.

> **Condensers.** If a condenser is undersized or dirty, the head pressure and condensing temperature rise. The higher temperature will make the compressor pump to this higher pressure and temperature. It is important to check and clean condensers regularly.

Refrigeration system troubleshooting

Few boats carry vacuum pumps, bottles of refrigerant, gauge sets and spare parts. In fact to carry out refrigeration work may be a breach of environmental laws if you are not certified. Knowingly releasing Class I (CFC) and Class II (HCFC) substances into the atmosphere can result in severe penalties and imprisonment. Besides working on refrigerator ships I used to work for a while as a refrigeration mechanic repairing shipping container systems. All my repairs were done in filtered clean areas. It is highly unlikely that conditions will be suitable for you to properly overhaul and repair compressors. There are few exceptions, and these are largely limited to professional refrigerator mechanics.

The best way to avoid problems is to have the system properly installed in the first place. This chapter does not include procedures for the disassembly and checking of compressors, purging and recharging, as you are more likely to do further damage. If after checking the control systems you are unable to rectify problems, call in a licensed refrigeration technician. It is important to determine what is going on in the system. Pressure gauges are used to check system pressures, and thermometers are used to measure evaporator, line and condenser temperatures.

Pipework joints

Refrigerant oil is always circulating in a refrigeration system along with the refrigerant. When a leak is observed at a connection this needs to be tightened.

When tightening fittings, always carefully tighten the fitting about ¹⁄₁₆" (1.5mm) of a turn. Check for leaks before tightening again. It is common to over tighten these fittings which may be flared style or have integral O-rings. Over tightening often damages the rings or distorts the pipe flares causing leaks.

There are recommended fitting torque values and you should always check the suggestions found in the manufacturers' installation manuals.

Refrigeration system maintenance

There are a number of maintenance tasks that will help keep the refrigeration system function properly.

Weekly Checks

Always check the evaporator or the holding plate for excess frost build-up. This ice will restrict the airflow through the chest and affect cooling efficiency.

When ice build-up thickness reaches ½" (12mm) in thickness you should defrost the unit. It is best to do it more frequently. I do so at just ¼" (6mm) thickness.

To defrost, turn the refrigerator unit off and wait for about 60 minutes and remove all food and drinks. You can use an automotive windshield ice scraper to help dislodge the ice. You can also pour on warm or hot water to the ice surface to help thaw it out for removal.

I have often seen people use screwdrivers and ice picks or other sharp tools to remove the ice. This is dangerous and many times it has resulted in a punctured evaporator and a big repair bill.

As a hint you can spray on food grade liquid grease and I know some who spray on a light coating of cooking oil. This is to prevent ice build-up attaching itself to the evaporator or the holdover tank surfaces.

Monthly Checks

Check moisture indicators and where saturated change the dryer.

Six-monthly Checks

Seawater cooling condensers should be cleaned where this is possible. Where systems have anodes in the cooler they should be checked and replaced.

Inspect all electrical wiring and wiring terminals and check tighten.

Check that all mechanical brackets are tight and there is no movement.

Visually inspect system for corrosion on the compressor housing. Also check for saltwater on water cooled systems as this may cause corrosion of the aluminum casings. Seawater will also degrade copper tubing and crack any O-rings, which in turn will cause leaks and system failure.

Annual Checks

Change the dryer every year if there is no moisture indicator to show condition.

Inspect compressor carbon brushes and replace if low or well worn.

Check all hoses for chafe and wear and general condition. Some manufacturers recommend a total replacement every 10 years.

Water condenser maintenance

One problem with seawater cooled condensers is that an alkaline scale tends to accumulate on the condenser. This is often indicated by a compressor that runs a lot longer than normal and sometimes the high pressure cut-out switch trips.

On many refrigeration systems the condenser can be maintained relatively easily, by using either mechanical or chemical methods. The methods are not unlike cleaning engine cooling systems. First you have to remove the condenser end caps. Then you gently pass a wooden dowel through each of the tubes to dislodge scale. I have used brass gun cleaning style brushes to clean the tubes thoroughly. On the Sea Frost systems you need to remove the zinc then plug the bottom hole. Next you remove the top hose and add 6oz (177ml) of muriatic acid solution with a ratio at around 5% to 7%.

This will cause foaming to start as it reacts with the scale and when this stops reconnect the hose, open the through-hull valve and start the system. Run for a few minutes to ensure that the system is completely flushed through. Stop the system and close the through-hull valve, reinstall the zinc and place the system back in service.

Refrigerant loss

Refrigerant loss is the most common fault. It causes a gradual reduction in cooling efficiency, eventually trips the low pressure cut-out (if fitted), and the system fails. Low refrigerant levels can be observed in the sight glass; bubbles will be seen. An empty sight glass indicates no refrigerant at all. If all the gas has escaped, after the leak has been located, the system must be purged of air and moisture before being recharged. Normally, you should get a qualified and reputable refrigeration mechanic to do this.

If the system is undercharged, the refrigerant does not properly liquefy before passing through the TX valve, effective latent heat is reduced so refrigeration is poor. Some vapor will pass through the TX valve reducing refrigerator control capacity, and the vapor passing at high velocity will increase the wear on the TX valve needle and seat. Air in the system will increase total head pressure. Total head pressure equals refrigerator condensing pressure plus air pressure in the condenser. The refrigerant will then have to condense to a higher temperature and pressure. The cylinder head and exhaust on compressor and top tube of the condenser will all be at higher temperatures. This will then affect the oil quality. It is also important to ensure that caps on service valves are replaced and tight to reduce leaks.

Leak detection

The most common causes of leaks within refrigeration systems are at connection points. Always check all these points when leak detecting a system.

Leaks are easy to locate. If you suspect a leak, apply a soap-water solution and watch for bubbles forming on these connections. Use a flashlight and a small mirror (e.g., dental mirror) to examine the underside of connections. Also, wipe all connections with your finger.

Perform leak detection by pressurizing the system and checking all possible leakage locations at joints and fittings. Do not use a halide torch with HFC-134a refrigerants.

Halide torch

The most common test requires the use of a halide torch. Air is drawn to the flame through a sampling tube. Small gas leakages will give the flame a faint green discoloration, while large leaks will be bright green.

Soapy water

A simple method is to apply soapy water, generally dishwashing liquid, to all piping joints with the system running. If a pressurized leak is in the joint, a bubble will form.

Refrigeration system installation

There are kits for DIY refrigeration installations, however the best practice is to get a good refrigeration mechanic to install the system. A number of factors can be controlled.

Insulation

If a refrigerator system is to be effective and reliable, it must be of sufficient size to meet the expected needs, and be well insulated. Insulation thicknesses should be at least 4 inches or more. Inadequate insulation levels cause for inefficient boat refrigeration systems. Install as much insulation as you can. Every insulating material has varying degrees of thermal conductivity. The ideal insulating material is urethane foam, followed closely by fiberglass wool and polystyrene foam. In many installations, foaming is done in place using a two-part mix, but great care must be taken, as failure to have the mix correct will produce inadequate results, without a good closed cell finish that is required for good insulation. Ideally, the use of preformed slabs is much more reliable, and fill any outstanding voids with foam mix. The whole insulation block should be surrounded with plastic to prevent the ingress of moisture, with a layer of reflective foil such as that used in house construction to minimize heat radiation. A two-layer system of foam slabs and foil is the ideal combination. Vacuum insulation panels are a good investment.

Many refrigeration manufacturers offer thermal insulation panels. These can be retrofitted relatively easily into an existing box as long as sufficient space exists and the box lid is large enough for access. The panels from Technautic are 1" (2.5cm) thick and are approximately equal to around 4" (10cm) of closed-cell urethane foam insulation. The Glacier Bay Barrier Ultra-r vacuum insulation panel are rated at R-50 per inch (per 2.5cm) insulation value. This is equal to around 10" (25cm) of closed-cell urethane foam.

An area often overlooked is the entry and exit points of system tubing into the box. Ensure that these points are well insulated and sealed. A sure sign of leaks can be excessive run times of compressors and excessive ice up of the evaporator or holding plate.

Another popular point is the seal on the lid. On any refrigerator system always check that the seal is totally efficient. Some use the paper test and slide a banknote around the entire lid to see if it will slide in and to check that the lid is sealing tightly. Some manufacturers offer ready-made hatch insert with lids that are guaranteed to seal and close properly.

Freestanding refrigerators

Freestanding refrigerators and freezer combination units designed for boats are becoming almost standard on many new boats both power and sail. They can be front or top loading. They all use Danfoss BD35F compressors and 134a refrigerants and operate off 12 or 24 volts DC power or AC power. Typical power consumption is only 3.3 amps to 3.7 amps.

They have stainless steel interiors and many have lock systems to prevent accidental opening under boat movement and a vent system when not in use to prevent mildew.

Many small boats opt for portable refrigerators. I have one myself which is excellent.

Home refrigerators

Many boats have home freestanding type refrigerators installed. Maintain by keeping clean and deodorized to avoid smells.

Refrigerator Not Cooling Or Not Coming Down to Temperature

The usual cause is that the thermostat is set incorrectly or is malfunctioning. Check that the hermetic compressor is actually operating. If it is running there may be a compressor fault, or a loss of gas in the system. Heavy ice or frost build up on the evaporator coils will also seriously affect cooling and require defrosting, and this may indicate an automatic defrost problem. Condensers must be kept clean. Dust accumulates when fan cooling is used, and heavily clogged condensers will require cleaning. If a fan is installed always check that the fan is operating. If the refrigerator is badly ventilated this can also affect the cooling function. In some cases the refrigeration does not start after a defrost cycle.

Refrigerator Builds Up with Frost

Most units have automatic defrost systems. If the defrost timer is malfunctioning, or the defrost heater or thermostat is not functioning correctly frost will build up. If after manual defrosting the system cools correctly then the auto defrost system has failed.

Freezers

Upright and top loading freezers are often installed in vessel galleys. Symptoms and causes for failure are similar to those in refrigerators.

The Freezer Is Not Functioning

The most common causes are the power is off, the thermostat is faulty, the defrost timer is malfunctioning, or the compressor is faulty. If the compressor is running this may also be due to refrigerant loss.

Cooling Is Reduced

Check the condensers, which must be kept clean. Make sure the fan is running. Check for excess ice build up on the evaporator. The thermostat if faulty may cycle off too early.

2. ICE MAKERS

Ice makers are on many motor and power boats. Systems are available in 12 volts and also in 110/220 volts AC. The refrigeration system principles remain the same and systems should be maintained. Water filters should be installed and regularly checked and cleaned.

No Ice Production or Ice Production Has Stopped

Check that the machine power is on. If the wire adjacent to the ice maker is raised, lower the wire to restart. Check that fill tube is not blocked with ice, and a hair dryer is useful in defrosting this. Check that the water filling valve and shutoff valves are functioning.

Small Ice Cube Production

The most common cause is a clogged water inlet pipe, or the water inlet valve is faulty. The next probable cause is the thermostat is faulty. If the refrigeration is not functioning correctly this will also affect ice cube production.

Fishermen's ice box systems

Crushed ice is preferred by fishermen as it refrigerates the new catch more quickly. The Dometic Eskimo Ice system can produce up to 600 pounds (272kg) of crushed ice per day. That is 25 pounds (11.3 kg) of ice per hour. Generally these are mounted below deck and the crushed ice is pumped through hoses to the fish box or cooler.

Remote systems have a typical power consumption of 14 amps for the condensing unit, 2 amps for the auger unit for 155 VAC systems and half that for 230 volt systems. Self contained units typically consume 16 amps for 115VAC and 600 lb per day systems. Dometic also market a smaller 250 lb per day unit.

Ice maker troubleshooting

Ice Maker Not Starting

Power supply is switched off

Circuit breaker has tripped

Loose connection or switch fault

Refrigeration controller faulty

Compressor relay is faulty or not operating

Icemaker module is faulty

Insufficient Cooling to Make Ice Cubes

Refrigerant leakage

Condenser is clogged

Refrigeration compressor is faulty

Fan motor is faulty or jammed

Icemaker control module is faulty

No Water Supply to Make Ice Cubes (but Freezing)

Water filter is clogged or the water supply is off

Water inlet solenoid is faulty or seized

Mold heater assembly is faulty

Icemaker module is faulty

Refrigeration controller is faulty

No Ice Cube Ejection

Ice mold thermostat is faulty

Icemaker module is faulty

Ice ejection relay is faulty

Machine Stops in Mid-Ejection Cycle

Icemaker control module is faulty

Electrical connection fault

Ice ejection relay fault

Electrical power supply fault

Slow Ice Production Rate

Ice mold thermostat is faulty

Condenser is clogged

Fan motor is faulty

Ice ejection relay is faulty

Excess Water and Ice Accumulations

Water inlet solenoid valve is faulty

Icemaker control module is faulty

Ice mold thermostat is faulty

Water filling assembly is misaligned

3. AIR CONDITIONING

Air conditioning is possible on even small boats and is virtually standard on larger vessels. Like refrigeration, air conditioning cools a cabin by transferring heat out. In most marine installations, seawater is used generally for condenser cooling although fan cooled systems are available but they are less effective. There are two types of marine air conditioning system, the single stage direct expansion and the tempered (chilled) water two-stage type.

Systems are generally rated in British thermal units (BTU) which is the energy required to heat or cool an area. In metric this is Kilo calories (Kcal). The conversion is approximately 4 BTU = 1Kcal. Systems requiring gas charging must be performed by certified technicians and use approved (EPA) equipment.

Self contained and remote condensing systems

These single stage direct expansion units may be either self-contained or have a remote condensing unit installed within the machinery space. The self-contained reverse cycle system is normally a relatively compact module, such as the Cruisair StowAway, that can be installed under a bunk or locker. These are rated between 5,000–24,000 BTU/hr.

They are pre-charged with R-22 refrigerant at the factory, are seawater cooled from a remote pump, and have integral reciprocating, rotary or scroll compressor depending on the model. Units also have integral condenser, evaporator, blower, safety switches etc. Many systems have a remotely installed condensing unit within the machinery space, with seawater supply also adjacent. Refrigerant is carried to the air-cooling unit. These units have cooling capabilities in the range 5,000 to 60,000 BTU/hr.

Figure 3.1 Air Conditioning Schematic

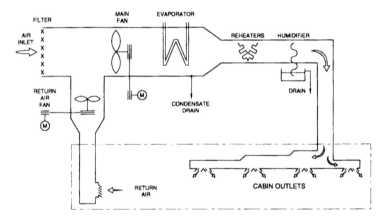

System components

Air Handling Units

For efficient air conditioning these need to be properly designed. They contain air plenum chambers along with coils and tubing. Many air handling units employ quiet and efficient centrifugal blowers. Some units now have brushless DC motors that use speed control for quiet operation. Also they have condensate drains and quality units are also fully insulated to prevent condensation forming.

Control System

This may be a simple thermostat or a more sophisticated multi function device with digital readouts and more.

Powering an air conditioning using the boat generator is always a major consideration. In many cases when the compressor cycles the start-up current causes a spike that makes lights flicker and often audible loading of the generator. Once a compressor starts the running current is significantly lower. Dometic have a unit called SmartStart that reduces start-up power demand. These type of units are also known as soft start units and could make a difference with installing a very expensive larger generator.

Electrical power requirements

AC Powered Systems

A system normally requires a constant AC power source to operate, so the generator must run continuously. Cruisair quote as a guide 1 amp per 1,000 BTU/hr, however 1.3 is closer for 117 VAC systems. If an air conditioning system is to be installed on the vessel the generator must take account of the maximum loads. As systems use AC induction motors on the compressor there is a significant start-up current surge that must be allowed for in generator load calculations, typically 3–4 times full-load amps. Hermetically sealed compressors have high starting currents that are reduced by capacitors to around 3–5 times running current.

Seawater Pumps

Electrical load calculations should also factor in the seawater pump. Pumps are generally not self-priming and must be positioned at or below water line. Like all seawater pumps they are prone to corrosion. Self-priming impeller pumps should be installed where possible. The seawater pump is generally controlled via a relay box, and this should be mounted in a dry location. Pump capacities are typically 100gph for a 5,000BTU unit up to 250gph for a 12,000BTU system.

DC Powered Systems

The Marine Air Systems (Dometic) 12 DC system is an example of recent systems. It has a hermetically sealed compressor and draws 29 amps for a 3,500 BTU/h (750Kcal/h) unit so the engine may have to run to supply the power, and an additional alternator is a good option.

Control Systems

Controls range from simple on and off switches, speed control and thermostat to programmable controllers. These offer timing functions; high and low temperature settings, systems monitoring, fan speed controls and compressor restart time delays, including fault condition automatic shutdown and even automatic dehumidification. Protection and control systems are similar to those in refrigeration systems. There are also variable speed fan controllers that use small variable frequency drives.

Capacity Calculations

The capacity of the system must be calculated by determining the volume to be cooled. The following are guidelines used by HFL. For ambient temperatures exceeding 30°C add 20%, and for water temperatures exceeding 25°C add a further 20%. This is to maintain 16–22°C. The estimated seawater-cooling requirement is for 3.5 gallons per minute for each self-contained unit.

For below decks cu.ft x 14 = BTU. (m^3 x 504 = BTU).

For above decks cu.ft x 17 = BTU. (m^3 x 612 = BTU).

Air Conditioning Capacity Table

Capacity (BTU/hr)	Below Deck Sq. Ft	Mid Deck Sq. Ft	Above Deck Sq. Ft
6000	90	60	45
7000	115	75	55
9000	165	110	85
12000	200	150	100
16000	267	178	135
20000	335	250	167
24000	405	300	200

Tempered (chilled) water systems

Tempered water systems are used on larger boats and commercial vessels. A chiller refrigeration unit is used to chill (or warm in reverse cycle systems) water, which is then circulated around the vessel by a freshwater circulating pump through insulated piping in a closed loop to the fan coil air-handling units. A seawater system is also used to cool the condenser.

Modular installation materials from companies such as Climma have special purpose color coded flexible piping, valves, fittings etc., that simplify installation. Systems such as those from Dometic and Cruisair have modular control systems, which incorporate temperature control, control circuits to pumps and refrigeration compressors, fault alarm indicators, and systems monitoring.

Chilled water systems have water flow loss alarms and shutdowns, and high and low temperature limits, that prevent either freezing or overheating of the water. A time delay relay for the compressor contactor may also be installed to prevent all auxiliaries such as water pumps and air handling units powering up together, which reduces electrical load surges. Tempered water systems should be checked regularly for leaks and to make sure that the water level is adequate to prevent air in the system. Air handler motorized valves should be checked for corrosion and lubricated periodically.

Most now have programmable control systems, which use a replaceable plug-in EPROM for the program. The system has a non-volatile memory to retain settings when off. System controls offer various features that include automatic dehumidification, intermittent or continuous fan operation, low and high fan speeds and operating temperature differentials. The air handlers require a power/logic module and temperature sensing elements. The controllers have integral LED digital displays that also show fault codes, program prompts and temperature information.

Some manufacturers are now using Variable Frequency Drives (VFD) on compressors to eliminate the large starting inrush current of the compressor. These are used to ramp up voltage and frequency in a controlled time period. The important feature is that they allow operation on limited dockside power, and as well protect the generator from overload. In addition the VFD will also run a 60Hz rated compressor at 60Hz, even when input power is 50Hz, which allows full BTU capacity performance in foreign places. The drive also protects the compressor by monitoring input voltage and output current, and will shut it down if there is a power supply problem. The VFD unit produces a modified sine wave output for smooth acceleration and running, with precise frequency control.

Chilled water system maintenance

There are a number of maintenance tasks to be performed.

Weekly Checks. Check the seawater inlet strainer and clean.

Monthly Checks. Filters on air cooling units should be checked and cleaned.

Six-monthly Checks. Seawater cooling condensers should be cleaned where this is possible. Where systems have anodes in the cooler they should be checked and replaced.

Air conditioning troubleshooting

Air conditioning systems have many faults similar to refrigeration systems.

Check external control equipment such as thermostats.

Check system HP and LP cut-outs where installed.

Check evaporator cooling systems are clean and functioning.

Chilled water systems troubleshooting

Low Water Flow

The circulation pump is either faulty or has tripped off. If the pump is operating check that the pump has not become air locked. This may require the opening of the system at the fill valve point and bleeding the system. If pressures are normal the flow switch may have failed.

Compressor Not Running

Check power supply and circuit breakers. Check control devices such as thermostats, and the liquid line solenoid valves. Check HP and LP cut-outs are not activated. LP faults can be caused by reduced refrigerant, and gas pressures should be checked and leak points identified.

High Discharge Pressure

The condenser is the usual cause, and it may be plugged, or have insufficient cooling water passing through it, or more commonly the strainer is clogged with weed or other debris. Systems with air cooled condensers may have been clogged or the fan is not operating.

Low Suction Pressure

It may be due to low water flow, as well as a clogged filter/dryer, and this requires replacement. A dirty evaporator and low refrigerant charge levels are also a cause and the system should be checked for leaks. Expansion valve problems may also create the problem.

Freeze Protection Operates

This is due to a faulty or incorrectly set freeze thermostat. Low chilled water flow can also cause this and should be checked. Check that any strainers within the system are not clogged. The other possible cause is low suction pressure.

Compressor Loading and Unloading Not Operating Properly

The main cause is a faulty or an incorrectly set thermostat. Another cause is a flow switch fault or low water flow. The capacity controller may also be at fault, or the unloading mechanism.

Figure 3.2 Climma chilled water system

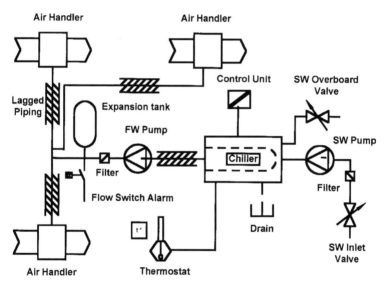

4. HEATING SYSTEMS

Many air conditioning systems are also capable of heating. On many boats in cold climates, however, a separate heating system is required. Diesel heating systems are very popular and having had these on two boats I was very happy to extend my boating all year round.

Typical systems include those from Webasto, Eberspacher and Mikuni which are very compact and generate considerable amounts of heat. I used to live on an old Dutch barge in Europe for several years and used a Dutch Kabola diesel fired central heating system which I was very happy with. These manufacturers also make diesel hot water systems as well.

Diesel hot water boilers

Some larger boats have a more substantial oil fired boiler system, and steam boilers have similar principles. The Kabola and Hurricane are typical units. Boilers provide hot water for air conditioning heating, hot water, and central heating. The Hurricane unit can burn No.1 and 2 diesel, kerosene and furnace oil. Installation is critical and the exhaust system must be properly specified and installed. Good combustion depends on good drafting, so the length, diameter and limited bends all affect this.

The thermostat is used to set the required temperature setting and is the set-point. The power switch is turned on which initiates the ignition cycle.

The oil burner unit fan starts and purges the boiler of fumes. Oil is then injected from the boiler nozzle, and ignited using a piezo ignition device. If the flame stops the system is shutdown by a flame failure device for safety.

Exhaust gas is taken outside via the flue. Electric ignition current draw is typically around 2 amps for 30 seconds. Kabola units on 24 VDC have a jet atomizing burner unit with an oil preheating element, and a typical start-up power consumption of 4 A and 5-7 A during operation.

Depending on which service is selected, i.e. hot water, central heating etc., the inlet water solenoid valve opens, and the circulating pump starts operating. The cold water inlet is solenoid controlled and is regulated by a flow valve. The system has a pressure relief valve installed.

The hot water is heated via a heat exchanger and when the set-point temperature is reached, the thermostat controls burner operation to maintain it. Typically this should be around 180°F (82°C). Overheat cut-outs should be set at approximately 195°F (91°C).

Troubleshooting heaters

The usual problems on any oil burner system are the burner ignition points or glow plugs. Burners tend to require regular cleaning as they can clog or soot up, and atomization affects the efficiency. Flame failure devices also require regular cleaning. Solenoid valves can stick and should be checked. The usual electrical faults of poor connections are common, as maintenance tends to be a lot lower because people avoid the dirty and often carbonized boiler.

An oil filter unit should be installed, and checked regularly (clean oil is essential for good operation). High temperatures or failure to ignite often indicate thermostat failures, so check this before going into burner control circuits. If the central heating radiators are not getting warm check the circulation pump supply first, and if the pump is functional check the heating and control circuits.

Diesel air heater operation

Typical power consumption figures, heat outputs and fuel consumption rates for typical Eberspacher models are illustrated in the table. Heaters have the following operational cycles:

Starting. An electric fan draws in cold air to the exchanger/burner. In most systems there is an air purge period.

Ignition. Fuel is drawn at the same time by the fuel pump, mixed with the air, and ignited in a combustion chamber by an electric glow plug.

Combustion. The combustion takes place within a sealed exchanger and gasses are exhausted directly to atmosphere.

Heating. Heat is transferred as the main airflow passes over a heat exchanger to warm the outlet air to the cabin. A thermostat in the cabin shuts the system down and operates to maintain the set temperature.

Typical Diesel Heater Data Table

BTU Output	Fuel (liters/hour)	Power Draw
6100	0.21	40 watts
11000	0.38	45 watts
15000	0.57	70 watts
28000	1.05	115 watts
41000	1.40	190 watts

Power consumption

Typical power consumption is 40 watts (3.33 amps) during running. At start up the draw can be up to 20 amps for a period of 20 seconds during the glow plug ignition cycle.

Figure 4.1 Diesel Heater System

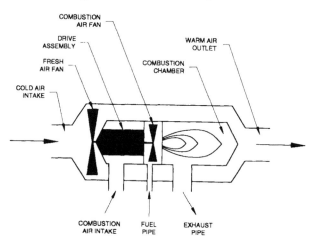

Heater maintenance

The following maintenance tasks should be carried out to ensure optimum operation:

1. Check that all electrical connections are tight and corrosion free.

2. Check exhaust connections and fittings for leaks. Leakages can cause dangerous gases to vent below deck.

3. Remove and clean the glow plugs. Take care not to damage glow plug spiral and element. Use a brush and emery cloth, and ensure all particles are blown out afterwards.

4. At 2,000 hours, take the unit to the dealer and have the heat exchanger de-coked and the fuel filter replaced.

Diesel heater troubleshooting

Heater Will Not Switch Off

Temperature switch fault

Heater Smokes and Soots

Combustion pipe is clogged

Fuel metering pump fault

Blower speed is too low

Heating Level Too Low

Hot air ducts are clogged

Fuel metering pump fault

Blower speed is too low

Temperature switch fault

The Heater Will Not Start

Supply fuse has blown—replace

Low battery voltage—check battery charging

Blower is not operating

Fuel metering pump fault

Thermal cut-out tripped—reset

Fuel filter is clogged—change the filter

No fuel supply—check supply valve

Glow plug fault

Control unit fault

Heater Goes Off

Fuel metering pump has a fault

Thermal cut-out has tripped

Fuel filter has clogged

Fuel supply problem

There is a control unit fault

5. VENTILATION SYSTEMS

Good ventilation is essential in many areas of the vessel, which include the galley, machinery spaces and cabins. There are a number of ventilation fan options, and all have uses in particular applications. Fans can be classified either as extraction or supply (blowers) fans.

Extraction fans

Extraction fans take air out of a space, either to increase natural ventilation flow rates and air changes, or to remove excessive heat or fume concentrations.

Solar Fans

Solar fans are an excellent accommodation ventilation option. They simply have a small solar cell powering the fan motor. Some models have a small battery so that operation can continue at night after the fan has been charged by the solar module, which is the period when it is most required.

Engine Extraction Fans

These are used to extract heat from engine spaces. In warmer climates it is preferable to leave the fan operating for half an hour after the engine stops to reduce heat and stop lower deck temperatures increasing from the radiated engine heat.

Ventilators

The most familiar of these types are the Ventair and Ventilite static ventilators, the latter allowing natural light from the outside to come into the cabin. These units have two speeds and are reversible which allows adaptation to the conditions inside. Air displacement is very good at 25 CFM, which suits normal cabin environments. Power consumption is also relatively low at only 1.7 amps on the fast setting. A more economical option is the 2 speed VETUS units, which utilize an electronic brushless motor with a current draw of only 0.2 amps. Air extraction rates are a reasonable 36 CFM.

Blowers

Blowers supply or push air into a space, and are used to either displace existing air such as in bilge blower applications, or as in most cases to direct air in large volumes over specific areas. Ratings are either in m^3/min or Cubic Feet per Minute (CFM), with m^3/min = 250 CFM.

In-Line Blowers

In-line blowers are commonly used in bilge blower applications. These types simply install directly into the ventilation ducting tubes. Airflow rates are typically around 4–8 m^3/min and have a power consumption of around 4 amps.

Bilge Blowers

Bilge blowers are designed to operate in hazardous environments, and where hazardous vapors are concentrated they must be ignition proof. They are often used to ventilate engine spaces. Typical airflows are in the range of 150–250 CFM. Power consumption is in the range of 4 to 10 amps, which is quite high. In most cases, they are run with the engine operating and it is a good practice to interlock the fan to the engine start with a relay to ensure that it always operates and switches off at engine shutdown.

INDEX

air conditioning systems
  AC powered, 58
  air handlers, 57
  capacity calculations, 60
  components, 57
  controls, 57, 59, 61
  DC powered, 59
  installation, 61
  maintenance, 63
  power requirements, 58
  remote, 56
  schematic, 56
  self-contained, 56
  single-stage, 55
  tempered water systems, 61–65
  troubleshooting, 63, 64–65
  two-stage, 55
  types, 55
alkylbenzene, 19
alarms
  water flow loss, 61
amp-hours
  freezer usage, 2, 15
  refrigerator usage, 2, 15
anodes, cooling system, 20, 25, 41, 63

batteries
  charging, 2, 3, 27
  low voltage, 23, 73
  maintaining voltage level, 37
  refrigeration demand, 2, 4, 5
belts, engine, 15, 16, 17, 20, 23, 38
blowers
  heating system, 73
  refrigeration system, 56, 57
  ventilation, 75, 77
boilers, hot water, 68, 69
British thermal units (BTUs), 55
  conversion to Kilo calories, 55

calorifier, 3
capacitators, 25, 30, 31, 32, 58
circuit breakers, 21, 23, 31, 36, 53, 64
climate, 2
  cold, 25, 67
  tropical, 26, 38, 75
Climma, 61
  chilled water systems, 65
clutches
  engine interlock, 36
compressors, 5
  brackets, 16
  Danfoss, 3, 25, 26, 27, 48
  drive belts, 16, 20
  eutectic system, 15
  hermetic, 25
  Isotherm Magnum ASU, 25, 27
  maintenance, 17, 20
  noises, 21, 33
  reciprocating, 3, 17, 18, 20
  refrigeration system, 6
  speed control, 27
  swash plate, 15, 17, 18
  troubleshooting, 21, 30–33, 39, 64, 65
  Variable Frequency Drives (VFD), 62
  ventilation, 37
  warm to touch, 29
  windings status, 30
condensers
  maintenance, 20, 38, 43, 50
  pressure, high/low, 21
  refrigeration system, 6
  undersized, 38
covers, food, 37
Cruisair, 85
  StowAway, 56
  system power guide, 58
  tempered water system controls, 61

Danfoss compressors, 3, 25 26, 27, 48
defrosting, 17, 41, 49, 51
  timers, 35, 49, 50
diesel
  heating systems, 67–74
  No. 1 and 2, 68
Dometic, 85
  Eskimo Ice system, 52
  Marine Air Systems, 59
  SmartStart, 57
  tempered water system controls, 61
dryer
  refrigeration system, 10, 11, 42

Eberspacher, 67, 85
  fuel and power consumption, 70
energy, saving, 37
Espar heating systems, 85
eutectic refrigeration systems, 13–15
  air versus water cooling, 14
  basic principles, 13
  compressors, 15
  holdover, 13, 38
exhaust, 17, 44, 68, 70, 72

fans, 37, 49, 61
  extraction, 75–76
  solar, 75
  ventilators, 76
freezer
  amp-hour usage, 2, 15
  freestanding, 48
  troubleshooting, 50
Freon, 12, 19
Frig-Mate, 37
Frigoboat, 85
  Smart Speed Control(SSC), 27
frost, 29, 35, 41, 65
  See also defrosting

General Electric, 25
generators, 5, 13, 57, 58, 62
Glacier Bay, 85
  DC motor systems, 15
  insulation, 46
  LS (low speed), 15
glow plugs, 69, 72

halide torch, 45
heating systems, diesel
  exhaust, 68
  fuel and power consumption, 70,
    71
  hot water boilers, 68
  maintenance, 72

operation, 70
thermostat, 68
troubleshooting, 69, 73–74
Hurricane heating systems, 68

ice makers
  fishermen's, 52
  power consumption, 52
  troubleshooting, 51, 53–54
  voltage, 51
insulation, 46–47
Isotherm, 85
  automatic start up (ASU), 25, 27
  self-pumping (SP) cooling systems,
    14

Kabola heating systems, 67, 68, 85
keel cooling, 14
Kenyon Marine, 85
kerosene, 68
Kiol calories (Kcal)
  conversion from BTU, 55
Kollman Marine, 85

Leeson, 15
lubricants, 18, 19
  See also oil

Mikuni heating systems, 67, 85
mineral oil, 19
motor, DC
  maintenance, 16
  systems, 16

Norcold, 85

oil
  compressor, 18, 28
  filter, 22
  low pressure, 22
  falling levels, 22
  low temperature, 23
  furnace, 68
  mineral, 19
  Polyalkylene Glycol (PAG), 19
  Polyol Ester, 19
  refrigerant, 40

pipework
  torque values, 40
Polyalkylene Glycol (PAG) oil, 19
Polyol Ester oil, 19
pump
  capacities, 58
  seawater, cooling, 14, 58

refrigerants, 6, 8
  charging, 28–29
  control, 7
  leakage, 24, 28–29, 40, 44, 45
  levels, 11
  pipework, 40
  regulations, 12, 28, 39
  types, 12
refrigeration systems
  amp-hour usage, 2
  auxiliary controls, 34–36
  battery power, 2
  compression, 6, 8
  condensation, 6, 8
  costs, 3, 4
  cut-out switches, 34
  cycle, 6–8
  diagram, 9
  dryer, 10, 11, 41
  dual system, 4
  electrical, 2, 3, 4, 16–20
  eutectic. *See* eutectic refrigeration
    systems
  evaporation, 7, 8
  frost, 29, 41
  holdover, 13, 38
  installation, 46–47
  lubricants, 18, 19
  maintenance, 41–43
  mechanical system, 2, 3, 4, 13
  pipework, 40
  power efficiency, 3, 27
  principles, 6
  selection, 2–5
  sight glass, 11, 29, 44
  troubleshooting, 21–24, 38, 39
refrigerators
  amp-hour usage, 2, 15
  freestanding, 48, 49
  troubleshooting, 49

Sea Frost systems, 43, 85
seals, testing, 47

seawater
  cooling, 14, 25, 38, 43, 55, 56, 60,
    61, 63
  corrosion, 42
  pumps, 58
  temperatures, 38
sight glass, 11, 29, 44
solar
  fans, 37, 75
  refrigeration systems, 4
switches, cut-out, 34

Technautics, 46, 85
temperatures
  boiling, 1
  Fahrenheit-Celsius conversion, 1
  freezing, 1
  low oil temperature, 23
  slow pull-down times, 23
thermostats, 35
  air conditioning, 57, 65
  heating system, 68
  refrigeration, 49
torch, halide, 45

valve, thermostatic expansion (TX),
    6, 7, 44
  failure of, 7
  servicing, 20
Variable Frequency Drives (VFD), 62
Veco air conditioning systems, 85
Ventair, 76
ventilation
  compressor, 37
  eutectic refrigeration, 14
  systems, 75–76
ventilators, 76
Ventilite, 76

Waeco Marine, 85
Wallas heating systems, 85
Webasto heating systems, 67, 85
windings, compressor, 30

ACKNOWLEDGEMENTS

Thanks and appreciation to the following companies for their assistance. Readers are encouraged to contact them for equipment advice and supply. Quality equipment is part of reliability!

Refrigeration
Dometic www.dometic.com
Waeco Marine www.waeco.com (Part of Dometic)
FrigoBoat www.frigoboat.com
Glacier Bay www.glacierbay.com
Isotherm www.isotherm.com
Kenyon Marine www.kenyonmarine.com
Kollman Marine www.kollmann-marine.com
Norcold www.thetford.com
Seafrost www.seafrost.com
Technautics www.technautics.com

Air Conditioning
Cruisair www.cruisair.com
Dometic www.dometic.com
Veco www.veco-na.com

Heating Systems
Eberspacher www.eberspacher.com/
Espar www.espar.com
Kabola www.kabola.nl
Mikuni www.mikuni.com
Wallas www.wallas.fi
Webasto www.webasto.com

Two major reference books by John C. Payne

Marine Electrical & Electronics Bible, 3E

More and more boaters are buying and relying on electronic and electrical devices aboard their boats, but few are aware of proper installation procedures or how to safely troubleshoot these devices when they go on the blink.

Now you can find all the information you need in this handbook. The author has put together a concise, useful, and thoroughly practical guide explaining in detail how to select, install, maintain, and troubleshoot all the electrical and electronic systems on a boat. This new edition is fully updated and illustrated with hundreds of informative charts, wiring diagrams and graphs.

"perhaps the most easy-to-follow electrical reference to date."
—*Cruising World*

"Everything a sailor could possibly want to know about marine electronics is here . . . as a reference book, it is outstanding."
—*Classic Boat*

Motorboat Electrical and Electronics Manual

This complete guide, which covers inboard engine boats of all ages, types and sizes, is a must for all builders, owners and operators.

"The book starts with the engine and works its way downstream, discussing everything from refrigeration and communications systems to heavy deck equipment and autopilots." —*Ocean Navigator*

"With today's growing interest in trawler and motorboat cruising, it is finally time for marine electrical systems to be explained in terms specific to the needs of the modern motorboat owner. Payne's book is one such resource. —*Passagemaker Magazine*

America's Favorite Sailing Books
www.sheridanhouse.com

Two practical books for every boater

Marine Diesel Engines
Maintenance and Repair Manual
Jean-Luc Pallas

The book covers the different engine parts and what they do, how the engine propels the boat, simple maintenance tasks, typical problem areas which can lead to a breakdown. Troubleshooting tables to enable you to diagnose the problem and fix it, and how to winterize your engine in your afternoon are also topics covered.

"Pallas explains the basic operation of marine diesel engines and describes essential techniques for their maintenance and repair. Color photographs and diagrams clearly illustrate each step. Most of the tasks described are within the abilities of the average boat owner and require no specialized equipment. Pallas is an instructor of recreational marine mechanics at La Rochelle Technical College in France." —*Sci-Tech Book News*

Outboard Motors
Maintenance and Repair Manual
Jean-Luc Pallas

The aim of this book, with its superb step-by-step photographs and detailed diagrams, is to enable every owner to understand the workings of an outboard motor (2 or 4 stroke) and be able to fix it with relative ease.

"This maintenance and repair manual provides everything you need to know about maintaining and fixing outboard engines. Simple maintenance tasks are covered along with problem areas and troubleshooting tables to help you diagnose problems. Step-by-step photographs and detailed diagrams help make it easy." —*Latitudes & Attitudes*

America's Favorite Sailing Books
www.sheridanhouse.com